# DONNA DEWBERRY'S
# Machine
# Embroidery
# FLOWERS

©2006 Donna Dewberry
Published by

**krause publications**
*An Imprint of F+W Publications*

700 East State Street • Iola, WI 54990-0001
715-445-2214 • 888-457-2873

Our toll-free number to place an order or obtain
a free catalog is (800) 258-0929.

The following trademarked terms and companies appear in this publication: Husqvarna™,
One Stroke™, Viking™, Cactus Punch™, Baby Lock, Bernina™, Brother®, Elna (USA),
Janome, Kenmore™, Sears®, Pfaff™, Simplicity®, Singer®, White®, Badger Basket Co.,
Dewberry Designs Inc., Prym™ Consumer USA, Springs Creative Products Group,
Sulky® of America, Blendables®, KK 2000™ Temporary Spray Adhesive, Teflon®,
Nancy's Notions®, Clotilde®, Ghee's®, QVC®, EZ® Quilting by Wrights®,
Creative Machine Embroidery, Designs in Machine Embroidery, Embroidery Journal,
One Stitch™, America Sews, HSN®, America's Store®, WonderFil®, Mettler®, Gütermann,
Cut-Away Plus™, Soft 'n Sheer™, Tear-Easy™, Totally Stable™, Sticky™, Stiffy™, Solvy™,
Super Solvy™, Ultra Solvy™, Paper Solvy™, Fabri-Solvy™, Heat-Away™, Puffy Foam™,
505® Spray and Fix, Schmetz.

Library of Congress Catalog Number: 2005934243

ISBN 13-digit: 978-0-89689-334-4
ISBN 10-digit: 0-89689-334-0

Designed by Heidi Bittner-Zastrow
Edited by Susan Sliwicki

Printed in The United States of America

# Acknowledgments

I want to thank some really hardworking and dedicated people for their involvement in this book. My heartfelt thanks to:

- Ethel and her friends, for all of their hard work to meet an impossible schedule with all of the projects to be completed.
- Julie and her sister, Carolyn, for all of their talent in making our patterns and projects look so great.
- Susan Sliwicki, my editor, for her love of her work; it shows!
- Viking and Cactus Punch, for supplying me with the necessary machines, the disk and their marketing team.
- All those others who I may not know, but who are instrumental in publishing and delivering this book.

Thank you all.

# Dedication

I dedicate this book to someone who has welcomed me into this industry with open arms and truly is a gracious and wonderful lady. She has such vision and energy, and her encouragement and faith in me has amazed me. I think we sometimes forget how wonderful people really can be, and then someone like Sue Hausmann comes into your life. Sue is truly amazing! Thank you, Sue.

# Introduction

As a native Floridian, I always have been surrounded by beautiful flowers. The name of my state is derived from the Spanish word for flower; it's certainly descriptive, because flowers grow in abundance in Florida year round.

Flowers have influenced my painting. But even before I became a painter, flowers decorated my life. When I was a teenager, my mother and I embellished clothing with our own designs. Now, as a mother of seven — including four daughters — I appreciate even more the value of adding decorative touches to articles of clothing to make them unique statements of individuality.

It's no secret that I've had a passion for decorative fabric painting for years. The idea of being able to "paint" those designs with the rainbow of beautiful threads is a new and exciting form of creative expression for me. The flowers, vines and insects included in this collection seem to come alive and jump right off of the clothing.

Through this book and the embroidery designs contained on the companion CD-ROM, I present many ways to create gifts, beautify your clothing and personalize your home décor. I hope that you enjoy this collection of designs I've put together.

*Donna*

# About the Author

Donna Dewberry loves anything to do with decorating, painting and crafting.

She is best known for her work in decorative painting. She is a frequent guest on HSN and its sister station, America's Store, and hosts her own PBS-TV show, "One Stroke Painting With Donna Dewberry." Donna also has designed a variety of fabrics for Springs Global, and has been a guest on the PBS-TV show "America Sews."

A prolific author, Donna has written or co-written a variety of how-to books about quilting, decorative painting and crafting with Krause Publications and North Light Books. Her titles include: "One Stitch Quilting: The Basics," "Donna Dewberry's Designs for Entertaining," "Papercrafting with Donna Dewberry," "Quilting With Donna Dewberry," "Donna Dewberry's All-New Book of One-Stroke Painting," "Flowers A to Z with Donna Dewberry," "Decorative Furniture with Donna Dewberry," and "Donna Dewberry's Complete Book of One-Stroke Painting."

# Table of Contents

# CHAPTER 1
# Machine Embroidery Basics

*Get your projects off to a great start
by learning a few basics of machine embroidery.*

*While this chapter touches on some key tools and techniques, there is much more information available. Your local embroidery machine dealer is a great resource for classes and reference materials.*

Carefully review the owner's manual for your machine, and seek out reference books, such as Jeanine Twigg's "Embroidery Machine Essentials" series and Nancy Zieman's "Machine Embroidery With Confidence," to learn more about machine embroidery.

## TOOLS

The right tools are essential to good machine embroidery work. Make sure you have these general embroidery tools ready to go for every embroidery project.

## Embroidery Machines

There are many embroidery machines on the market — everything from simple, embroidery-only basic machines to expensive machines with all of the bells and whistles.

While the options vary from machine to machine, some things are common to all embroidery machines.

You'll need a method to transfer the designs from the CD-ROM included with this book to your embroidery machine. There are several methods available. Some machines connect directly to a computer, while others can read from a floppy disk or a USB-port compatible memory stick. Others require a reader/writer box to write the design onto a card that fits your machine. In all cases, you'll need the proper software for your machine format. Visit your local machine dealer to find out what format your machine reads and what software and design transfer equipment you'll need. Once you have the necessary equipment, you can transfer the designs to your machine using the appropriate method.

Each machine reads a particular design format, which is noted by the file extension code on the end of the design file. You'll find the format for your machine in your owner's manual. The designs featured on the enclosed CD-ROM are created to work with

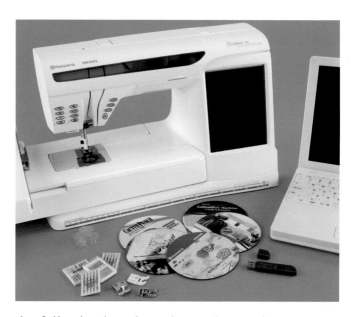

the following brands: Baby Lock, Bernina, Brother, Elna, Husqvarna-Viking, Janome, Kenmore, Pfaff, Simplicity, Singer and White.

## Needles, Pins and Clips

Just as in any other type of sewing, the needles used in machine embroidery are little pieces of equipment that make a big difference in how your projects turn out.

Always use needles that are made especially for machine embroidery. A machine embroidery needle has a larger hole that allows thread to pass back and forth through the eye of the needle with less wear on the thread. Choose the needle based on the design, type of thread and fabric you'll be using for the project. For example, if you plan to use metallic or specialty thread for embroidery, you should use a needle designed specifically for metallic thread; it has an even larger hole that prevents the metallic thread from fraying. When embroidering knits, such as T-shirts or sweatshirts, always use a ballpoint needle. Most importantly, change your needles often for the best results. See your owner's manual for detailed information.

You'll also want to keep pins handy to help keep fabrics positioned properly for embroidery. Typical sewing or quilting pins will work fine.

Clothespins or binder clips also will come in handy. Use these tools to keep the edges of your blanks or fabric out of the way during embroidery.

# Hoops

Embroidery hoops hold fabric in place for embroidery. The hoop attaches to the embroidery arm and moves the fabric under the needle to create the stitches.

The embroidery hoop comes in two parts: the outer ring, which connects the hoop to the machine; and the inner ring, which holds the fabric and stabilizer in place. The outer ring also has the adjustment screw that allows you to adjust the size to ease placing the fabric in the hoop.

Most embroidery machines come with a standard-size hoop that has a sewing field of approximately 4" x 4". Some machines accept larger hoop sizes;

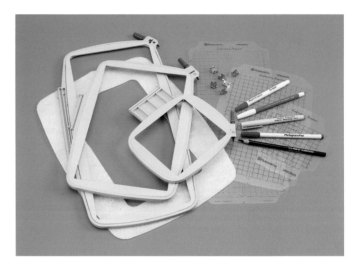

check with your local dealer for options.

If your machine only uses a 4" x 4" hoop, you may be unable to use the oversized designs that are included with this book. If you have not yet purchased an embroidery machine and are considering your options, remember that the ability to use a larger hoop provides you with a greater range of embellishment possibilities.

## How to Use a Hoop

**1.** Lay the outer ring on a flat surface. Place the stabilizer, which is cut larger than the hoop, and fabric on top of the hoop.

**2.** Place the inner hoop on the fabric; align the hoop marks. Match the main directional arrows, and align the fabric markings. Use both hands to press the hoop into place; position the right hand at the upper right corner and the left hand at the lower right corner.

**3.** Press until the hoop snaps into place. The fabric should be taut in the hoop. Don't pull the fabric, or you could distort its grain. If the fabric is too loose in the hoop, start the process over. Avoid tightening the hoop screw after the inner hoop has been set, because the fabric can become distorted and pucker.

**4.** Once the fabric and stabilizer are properly positioned in the hoop, place the hoop onto the machine. Keep the loose portions of the fabric from being under or over the hoop's embroidery field. To ensure that no loose edges get caught during embroidery, roll up the loose fabric outside of the hoop and secure it temporarily with binder clips or clothespins.

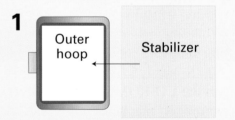

Position the stabilizer and fabric.

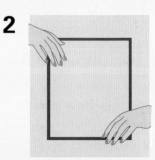

Hoop the layers.

Snap the hoops in place.

## Marking Tools

You'll want several marking tools to use with your templates. A template pencil may be provided with your machine. If not, purchase a template pencil in the notions department of your local fabric shop. You'll also want an eraser — a regular school-type eraser will do — and a water-soluble, erasable or removable marker. Be sure to test the marker on a scrap of fabric before using it on a project.

## Templates

Templates provided by embroidery machine manufacturers are plastic inserts that fit inside embroidery hoops. Usually, templates are printed with a grid, and often, they are notched so that they fit into the inner hoop in only one direction.

Using a template will ensure that your design is positioned correctly. If you don't have a template for your machine, check with your local dealer about ordering one, or make your own from transparency film, which is sold at office supply stores.

## Scissors

Whether you need to snip threads or cut stabilizer, good scissors are a must for machine embroidery.

Keep a sharp pair of close-cutting scissors in your work area to cut threads; curved-tip scissors often work well. If you have trouble opening and closing scissors, you can also get curved fine-tip snips that cut by gently squeezing. You'll also need standard scissors to cut away larger portions of stabilizer before using the smaller scissors for more refined areas. You'll want several pairs on hand, because stabilizer can quickly dull the blades.

## How to Use a Template

**1.** Before you start your project, use software to print out your chosen design, or stitch out your chosen design. Test-stitch the design using the threads you plan to use on your garment. This will give you a good idea of how the finished design will look.

**2.** Lay the plastic template over the paper copy or stitch-out. Center the design in the grid, which shows the embroidery field. If the design doesn't fit inside the grid, consider using a larger hoop, if possible. If the design is oversized and your machine only supports a 4" x 4" hoop, you won't be able to embroider the design on your machine. With proper software you may be able to split the design. Check with your local dealer to see if this is an option for your machine.

**3.** Once the design is centered, use the template pencil to outline the design on the template.

**4.** Use the template to place the design exactly where you want it on the project. Use the removable marker to mark the fabric at the registration marks or notches on the template. When hooping, align the fabric marks with the hoop inner ring marks to achieve precision design placement. When making multiple design placements, mark only one position at a time to avoid distortion.

**1**

Lay the template over the design.

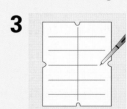

**3**

Outline the design.

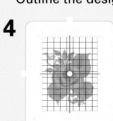

**4**

Position the design.

# SUPPLIES

## Stabilizers

The right stabilizer is one of the biggest keys to successful machine embroidery.

Stabilizer supports the stitches as they are placed on the fabric. An array of stabilizer categories, types and weights are on the market today, including cut-away, tear-away, mesh, fusible, liquid, water-soluble, water-activated, lofty and more.

Choose stabilizer based on the weight, type of fabric and end result desired. Always test-stitch first for the best results.

### Cut-Away Stabilizer

Cut-away stabilizer is used to stabilize the fabric during the embroidery process, but then is cut away from the back of the fabric once embroidery is complete. A small margin of stabilizer remains. Use cut-away stabilizers on delicate or unstable fabrics or knits.

### Disappearing Stabilizer

Disappearing stabilizers are temporary. They come in water-soluble, liquid or heat-removable formats in a variety of weights. Use disappearing stabilizer when you don't want any stabilizer left behind in your design after embroidery, such as when you're working with sheers or lace.

Some disappearing stabilizers also can be used as a topper over fabrics like terry cloth to prevent the nap of the fabric from poking through the stitches.

### Tear-Away Stabilizer

Tear-away stabilizer is temporary, and, as its name implies, it can be torn away from the motif after the embroidery process. Only the part of the stabilizer that is covered by the stitches stays in place.

When removing a tear-away stabilizer, gently pull the stabilizer away from the design edges. It's best to trim even tear-away stabilizers from delicate fabric.

### Spray Stabilizer

Spray stabilizers afford fabrics weight and support, but they wash out completely after embroidery.

Use spray stabilizer to stiffen a lightweight fabric, such as organza or voile, or to hold fabrics in place during the hooping process. Spray stabilizers come in an aerosol can or as a liquid in a pump-spray bottle.

## Spray Adhesives

Not to be confused with spray stabilizers, spray adhesives are used to hold multiple layers of stabilizer together, to hold pieces of appliqué fabric onto base fabrics or to hold toppers in place.

Never use sprays when the hoop is on the machine. Always set up a spray station away from the embroidery machine, such as in a cardboard box, to protect the machine from overspray and any possible damage. Set the hoop inside the box, and then spray.

# Threads

Most machine embroidery designs are digitized for use with 40-weight embroidery thread. Bobbin thread is used in the bobbin, unless it will show through, such as on a sheer fabric.

Always choose thread that is designed specifically for machine embroidery, and always test the thread first.

Included on the CD-ROM is a Thread and Design Guide for each design. If you want your designs to look exactly like the samples, use the colors indicated in the color chart. Even if your machine recommends thread colors, they may not be accurate; always use the thread chart from the CD-ROM unless another look is desired.

### Bobbin Thread

Bobbin thread is designed especially for machine embroidery. It holds the needle threads in place and is available in different weights. The color selection is somewhat limited, so match up dark thread to dark fabrics and light thread to light fabrics. The exception is when the bobbin stitching will show, such as on a sheer fabric. In this case, use a matching 40-weight thread in the bobbin.

### Cotton Thread

Choose cotton thread when you want a matte finish. Available in several weights, including a heavier 12-weight variety, cotton thread is often used in quilting or when an item is desired to have an antique look. Heavier threads are not recommended for the designs featured in this book.

### Metallic and Specialty Thread

Many metallic and specialty threads are available to add a designer touch to your machine embroidery.

Carefully choose how and when to use metallic and specialty threads. Some designs may be too dense to use specialty threads. Always use the proper needle with metallic and specialty threads, and always test them first.

### Polyester Thread

Polyester thread is a great choice for items that will be washed repeatedly, such children's clothing. A 40-weight polyester thread can be used to embroider any of the designs found on the companion CD-ROM included with this book.

### Rayon Thread

Both 30- and 40-weight varieties of rayon thread commonly are used for embroidery. Rayon thread has a sheen that looks good in most embroidery designs. For the majority of sample designs shown in this book, rayon thread was used, as the colors seem to stand out better.

# Blanks

Most of the projects in this book were created using purchased clothing and home décor items, such as garments, caps, aprons, towels and bedding. These are known as blanks.

Sometimes it's easy to open a shirt and lay it flat on an embroidery hoop. Other times — such as with embroidery around pant legs or jacket sleeves — a garment must first be taken apart at a seam to allow the leg or sleeve to lie flat enough to be hooped. After you embroider the design, use a matching all-purpose sewing thread to re-sew the seam.

In all cases, use blanks of your choice, select stabilizers appropriate for the fabrics, and choose stabilizer weights based on fabric weights. It's a good idea to purchase test fabric in a similar type and weight so you can test the designs and stabilizer choices before beginning your project.

# EMBROIDERY DESIGNS

The embroidery designs featured in this book are located on the CD-ROM included in the back of the book. You need a computer and compatible embroidery software to access and utilize the designs. They are: Damselfly; Hummingbird; Hydrangea 1; Hydrangea 2; Morning Glory, 5 x 7; Morning Glory, Bud; Morning Glory, Single; Rose, Large; Rose, Long; Rose, Trio; Leaves On Vine; Two Butterflies; Yellow Butterfly; Daisies; Iris; Tulips; Sweet Pea; and Pansies. A Thread and Design Guide and step-by-step instructions for eight Bonus Projects are located on the CD-ROM, too. You will need Acrobat Reader to view the files; this free, downloadable software is available at www.adobe.com.

## How to Use the CD-ROM Designs

**1.** To access the embroidery designs, insert the CD-ROM into the computer.
**2.** Locate the desired designs in the folder for each embroidery machine format. Copy the design files onto the computer hard drive using one of the operating system programs, or open the design in your embroidery software. Copy only the design format that is compatible with your brand of embroidery machine.
**3.** Once the designs are in your software or saved on your computer hard drive, transfer the designs to your embroidery machine by whatever means you normally use. For more information about using the designs with your software or embroidery machine, consult your owner's manual, or visit your local machine dealer.

## Create Your Own Arrangements

For many of the projects in this book, two or more design elements are combined to create the end result.

Combining designs can be accomplished in different ways. The most basic way is to use a template and embroider one design at a time. Some embroidery machines allow you to transfer more than one design to the machine and use the machine screen to move the designs around. Another way is to manipulate the designs with software.

Depending upon the software capabilities, you may be able to change the size of the design, add elements from one design to another or even add lettering to the design. Check with your local machine dealer to find out what types of software programs are available for your machine.

Another way to personalize the designs is to use different colors of thread than those listed in the Thread and Design Guide on the CD-ROM. Use your imagination: If you want a red rose instead of a pink one, choose different values of reds to replace the pinks. Or, try a design in a monochromatic family. Always use the colors that appeal to you.

# HELPFUL HINTS

Follow these helpful hints to make your machine embroidery easier and more enjoyable.

## Hold the Fabric in Place

Some embroidery machines have a special feature that helps to hold fabric in place while embroidering a design. It may be called "fix," "baste" or "outline." Check your owner's manual to see if your machine has this feature. This function creates a box of basting stitches the size of the embroidery field that will hold the fabric to the stabilizer. If your machine does not have this function, simply hand baste close to the hoop, or pin the item outside of the embroidery field.

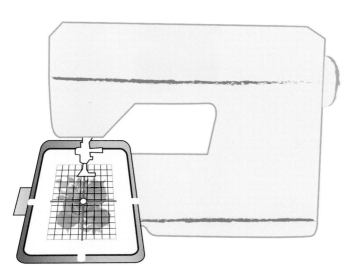

Use an outline, fix or baste function to hold the fabric in place.

## Check the Design Alignment

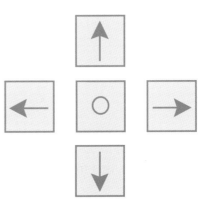

Adjust the alignment.

After placing the hoop on the embroidery machine, check to see that the design is centered with the needle in alignment with the design centering mark. The marked center point should be directly under the needle.

If it is available, use the design field check function to check the edges of the design field to make sure the design can be embroidered where placed. Check your machine manual for more information.

# Test-Stitch Designs

Embroidering a test stitch-out of designs is always recommended. You can check the stabilizer and fabric combinations and make any needed adjustments before you begin the project. When embroidering on ready-to-wear garments, find a fabric similar to the project fabric for testing.

Complete test stitch-outs.

# Plan the Design Placement

When you're adding a design to a garment you plan to wear, try on the garment first, and use a printed or stitched design template to help identify the right location for the design. Because all of us have different shapes and sizes, it's up to the individual to find the right place on a garment for a design.

When you're adding a design to a home décor item, think about how the item will be used. For example, if you place a design in the center of a place mat, the design will be hidden most of the time, unless you have clear plates.

Plan placement.

# CHAPTER 2
# Roses
## Signature Rose Denim Shirt

*Throughout the painting world, this rose has become my signature flower. There's just something about a rose that adds both romance and elegance to any background.*

## MATERIALS

### Supplies

Denim shirt

Cut-away stabilizer

Embroidery thread in rose pink, burgundy, dark rose pink, light rose pink, medium avocado green, dark khaki green, light avocado green and pale green

Bobbin thread

Temporary adhesive

### Tools

General tools listed in Machine Embroidery Basics

### Embroidery Designs

Rose, Large
Hummingbird

*Make an everyday denim shirt beautiful with these designs.*

# Denim Shirt Instructions

**1.**

Plan the design placement.

**1.** From the CD-ROM, print out the Thread and Design Guide for the Rose, Large. Outline the design on your hoop template. Lay the denim shirt out, and use the template to determine where to position the design on the shirt. For the sample shirt, the design was positioned above the left breast pocket by lining up the edge of the design with the edge of the pocket. Once you have the design in position, use the removable marker to mark the hoop placement guides, including the design center point.

**2.** Hoop the stabilizer, spray it with temporary adhesive, and adhere the shirt at the markings. If the denim is lightweight, hoop both layers.

**3.** Transfer the Rose, Large design to the machine.

**4.** Place the embroidery hoop on the machine.

**5.** Check that the design is centered with the needle in alignment with the design centering mark.

**6.** Use the "fix" or "baste" function to help hold the fabric in place.

**7.** Embroider the design. Refer to the Thread and Design Guide for the correct colors. Clip any jump stitches as you change thread colors. This will prevent the jump stitches from being sewn into the design.

**8.** When embroidery is complete, remove the hoop from the embroidery machine, and remove the shirt from the hoop. Remove the basting stitches or pins, and remove any excess stabilizer.

**9.** Repeat the embroidery steps to complete the hummingbird design on the shirt's front right side and left rear shoulder.

**10.** When embroidery is complete, remove the hoop from the embroidery machine, and remove the shirt from the hoop. Remove any basting stitches or pins, and remove any excess stabilizer.

# CHAPTER 3
# Hydrangeas and Butterflies
## Victorian Dresser Scarf

*Hydrangea bushes are wonderful shrubs;*
*the clusters of blossoms are bursting with delicate colors,*
*which usually attract a butterfly or two.*

*I love the look of antique linens on my furniture, and I love the flowers and butterflies on this linen place mat — two of my favorite things! This project is an example of how you can add embellishment to home décor items that you purchase. The motifs add just the right touch.*

# MATERIALS

## Supplies

Linen place mat with lace trim

Tear-away stabilizer

Embroidery thread in dark orchid, orchid, pastel orchid, variegated green, medium avocado green, dark khaki green, light avocado green, pale green, yellow and white

Bobbin thread

Temporary adhesive

## Tools

General tools listed in Machine Embroidery Basics

## Embroidery Designs

Two Butterflies
Hydrangea 1

# Dresser Scarf Instructions

**1.** From the CD-ROM, print out the Thread and Design Guide for the Hydrangea 1 design. Place the hoop template over the design template, and trace the outline with the template pencil. Use the template to decide where to position the hydrangea on the place mat. The hydrangea design was centered on the place mat shown.

**2.** Once you have the design position selected, use the removable marker to mark the hoop placement guides in the template, including the design center point.

**3.** Hoop the tear-away stabilizer and the place mat.

**4.** Transfer the Hydrangea 1 design to the machine.

**5.** Place the embroidery hoop on the machine. Make sure that the loose portions of the place mat are not under or over the sewing area of the hoop. Roll up the loose edges, and use binder clips or clothespins to secure them.

**6.** Check that the design is centered with the needle in alignment with the design centering mark.

**7.** Embroider the design. Refer to the Thread and Design Guide for details. Clip any jump stitches as you change thread colors. This will prevent the jump stitches from being sewn into the design.

**8.** Remove the place mat from the hoop, and cut away the excess stabilizer.

**9.** Select locations for the butterflies. Repeat the preparation and embroidery steps to add the butterflies to the dresser scarf. Use editing software or the machine screen, if available, to separate two butterflies. Place one on either side of the center hydrangea.

**10.** When embroidery is complete, remove the hoop from the embroidery machine, and remove the dresser scarf from the hoop. Remove any excess stabilizer.

**9.**

Use software to edit out one butterfly.

# CHAPTER 4
## Morning Glories
### Morning Glory Dress

*There's just something joyful about morning glories.
I love to step into my garden and see their blooms.*

*Brighten up a simple dress with beautiful blue morning glories.*

## MATERIALS

### Supplies

A-line dress with yoke

Appropriate stabilizer based on garment fabric

Embroidery thread in blue, bright navy, medium avocado green, dark khaki green, light avocado green, yellow and pastel yellow

Bobbin thread

Temporary adhesive

### Tools

General tools listed in Machine Embroidery Basics

### Embroidery Designs

Morning Glory, 5 x 7
Morning Glory, single

## Dress Instructions

**1.** From the CD-ROM, print out the Thread and Design Guide for the Morning Glory, 5 x 7. Place the hoop template over the design template, and trace the outline of the design with the template pencil. Lay the dress out and use the template to decide where to position the design. Note the placement of the design to avoid the bust points. Once you have the design in position, use the removable marker to mark the hoop placement guides, including the design center point.
**2.** Hoop the stabilizer and dress.
**3.** Transfer the Morning Glory, 5 x 7 design to the machine.

**4.** Place the embroidery hoop on the machine. Make sure that the loose portions of the dress are not under or over the embroidery area of the hoop. Roll up the loose edges, and use binder clips or clothespins to secure them.

**5.** Check that the design is centered with the needle in alignment with the design centering mark.

**6.** Use the machine's "fix" or "baste" function, if available, to hold the fabric in place.

**7.** Stitch the design. Clip any jump stitches as you change thread colors. This will prevent the jump stitches from being sewn into the design.

**8.** Remove the dress from the hoop; remove the basting stitches and any excess stabilizer.

**9.** Repeat as necessary to make a complete band across the bodice.

**10.** Transfer the Morning Glory, Single design to the machine. Repeat the template making and hooping instructions. Embroider a single morning glory bloom on the left shoulder of the dress as shown, or choose another location as desired.

**11.** When embroidery is complete, remove the hoop from the embroidery machine, and remove the dress from the hoop. Remove any excess stabilizer.

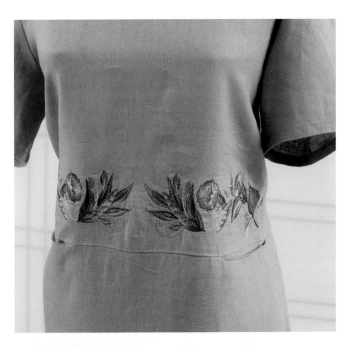

# CHAPTER 5
# Vines and Hummingbirds
## Hummingbird Dress and Jacket

*Hummingbirds are a special addition to any garden. I particularly love to paint these lovely pink and green creatures.*

*Add these designs to a dress to remind you of your garden.*
*A delicate vine down the center peeks through the open jacket,*
*while the hummingbird on the jacket front adds a charming accent.*

## MATERIALS

### Supplies

Sleeveless A-line dress and matching jacket

Appropriate stabilizer, based on garment fabric

Embroidery thread in avocado, green, dark khaki, petal pink, mauve, pastel yellow, dark khaki and white

Bobbin thread

Temporary adhesive

### Tools

General tools listed in Machine Embroidery Basics

### Embroidery Designs

Leaves on Vine
Hummingbird

## Dress Instructions

**1.** From the CD-ROM, print out the Leaves on Vine Thread and Design Guide. Place the hoop template over the design template, and trace the outline of the design with the template pencil. Lay out the dress, and use the template to decide where to position the design. On the dress shown, one design was centered vertically, just below the dress neckline, and additional vines were placed on either side of the slits. Once the design is in position, use the removable marker to mark the hoop placement guides in the template and the design center point.

**2.** If you are using a lightweight fabric, such as in the dress shown, use an adhesive tear-away stabilizer. Hoop the stabilizer, use a pin to score the paper backing inside the hoop perimeter, and peel away the paper to expose the adhesive. Adhere the dress on top of the stabilizer, and press it into place.

**3.** Transfer the design to the machine.

**4.** Place the embroidery hoop on the machine. Roll up the loose edges of the dress, and use binder clips or clothespins to secure them.

**5.** Check to ensure that the design is centered with the needle in alignment with the design centering mark.

**6.** Use the machine's "fix" or "baste" function, if available, to hold the fabric in place.

**7.** Embroider the design. Refer to the Thread and Design Guide. Clip any jump stitches as you change thread colors. This will prevent the jump stitches from being sewn into the design.

**8.** Repeat the preparation and embroidery steps to embroider additional vines as desired.

**9.** When embroidery is complete, remove the hoop from the embroidery machine, and remove the dress from the hoop. Remove the basting stitches and any excess stabilizer according to the manufacturer's directions.

# Jacket Instructions

**1.** Have the wearer try on the jacket before marking the design placement to find exactly where the Hummingbird should be located.

**2.** Repeat the template-making and hooping methods used for the dress.

**3.** Transfer the Hummingbird design to the machine. Refer to the thread chart for the suggested thread colors.

**4.** Embroider the Hummingbird onto the left lapel of the jacket or in another location as desired.

**5.** When embroidery is complete, remove the hoop from the embroidery machine, and remove the jacket from the hoop. Remove any excess stabilizer.

# CHAPTER 6
# Pansies
## Pansy Sweatshirt and
## Butterfly Turtleneck

*Pansies remind me of my grandmother, because they were her favorite flowers. I love adding pansies to my winter garden; their cheerful colors chase the winter blahs away.*

*This sweatshirt is the perfect way to bring warmth and joy to a cold winter day. The butterfly-accented turtleneck coordinates beautifully, and it adds a great finishing touch.*

## MATERIALS

### Supplies

Sweatshirt

Coordinating turtleneck shirt

Cut-away stabilizer

Paper-release, adhesive cut-away stabilizer

Embroidery thread in petal pink, bright yellow, mine gold, light purple, mauve, light rose, dark purple, mulberry, medium avocado green, dark khaki green, light avocado green, yellow, goldenrod, variegated green and pastel yellow

Bobbin thread

Temporary adhesive

### Tools

General tools listed in Machine Embroidery Basics

Ballpoint needle

### Embroidery Designs

Pansy
Yellow Butterfly

## Sweatshirt Instructions

**1.** From the CD-ROM, print out the Pansy design and the Thread and Design Guide. Place the hoop template over the design template, and trace the outline of the design with the template pencil.

**2.** Lay the sweatshirt out, and use the template to position the design. For the sample shirt, the design was centered about 4" below the neckline. If you are unsure about the placement, have the wearer put on the shirt, and place the design where it will look best. Once you have the design in position, use the removable marker to mark the hoop placement guides, including the design center point. If you're using a dark-colored sweatshirt, use a removable marker that will show on a dark fabric.

**3.** Hoop the cut-away stabilizer and the sweatshirt.

**4.** Change the embroidery machine needle to a ballpoint needle. Transfer the Pansy design to the machine.

**5.** Place the embroidery hoop on the machine. Make sure that the loose portions of the sweatshirt are not under or over the sewing area of the hoop. Roll up the loose edges of the sweatshirt, and use binder clips or clothespins to secure them.

**6.** Check that the design is centered so the needle is in alignment with the design centering mark.

**7.** Embroider the design. Refer to the Thread and Design Guide for correct colors of thread. Clip any jump stitches as you change thread colors; this will prevent the jump stitches from being sewn into the design.

**8.** When embroidery is complete, remove the hoop from the embroidery machine, and remove the sweatshirt from the hoop. Remove any excess stabilizer.

# Turtleneck Instructions

**1.** From the CD-ROM, print out the Yellow Butterfly design and the Thread and Design Guide.

**2.** Place the hoop template over the design template, and trace the design outline with the template pencil. Lay the shirt out, and use the template to decide where to position the design. For the sample shirt, the butterfly was placed on the collar just to the left of the center. Mark the center design position.

**3.** Hoop the paper-release adhesive stabilizer. Use the template to mark the center. Stick a pin straight through the center mark. Score the perimeter of the paper with a pin, and peel back the paper to expose the adhesive. The center mark will be visible, because you pierced the paper. Place the center mark on the collar at the center of the stabilizer and adhere the fabric.

**4.** Transfer the Yellow Butterfly design to the machine.

**5.** Place the embroidery hoop on the machine. Make sure that the loose portions of the turtleneck are not under or over the sewing area of the hoop. Roll up the loose edges, and secure them with clips or clothespins.

**6.** If the option is available on your machine, use the design rotation adjustment to turn the design in the right direction for your collar.

**7.** Use the machine's "fix" or "baste" function, if available, to hold the fabric in place. Otherwise, carefully pin outside of the embroidery field, or hand baste close to the hoop.

**8.** Embroider the design. Refer to the Thread and Design Guide for the correct colors of thread. Clip any

jump stitches as you change thread colors; this will prevent the jump stitches from being sewn into the design.

**9.** When embroidery is complete, remove the hoop from the embroidery machine, and remove the turtleneck from the hoop. Remove the basting stitches and the excess stabilizer; follow the manufacturer's directions.

# CHAPTER 7
## Daisies
### Lazy Daisy Baby Set

*Daisies always make me think of springtime when my garden is reborn. They also remind me of my grandchildren. They love to pick daisies from my garden and bring them to "Mima."*

*There is nothing more perfect for a new baby
than this gift set embroidered with daisies.*

# MATERIALS

## Supplies

One-piece knit baby garment

Bib

Receiving blanket

Mesh cut-away stabilizer

Paper-release adhesive tear-away stabilizer

Clear water-soluble stabilizer

Fusible knit tricot interfacing (optional)

Temporary spray adhesive

Polyester embroidery thread in off-white, mauve, petal pink, pastel mauve, bright yellow, mine gold, pale yellow, medium avocado, light avocado and dark khaki green

Bobbin thread

Temporary adhesive

## Tools

General tools listed in
Machine Embroidery Basics

Ballpoint needle

## Embroidery Designs

Daisies

# One-Piece Garment Instructions

**1.** Use the Daisies design, or use the resize feature of your embroidery machine or embroidery software to reduce the size of this design as desired. The sample design is reduced to one-quarter of its original size.
**2.** Print out the Daisies design and the Thread and Design Guide from the CD-ROM. Place the hoop template over the design template, and trace the outline design with the template pencil.
**3.** Lay the garment out, and use the design template to decide where to position the design. For the sample, the design is centered on the seat of the garment. Once the design is in position, use the removable marker to mark the hoop placement guides, including the design center point.
**4.** Hoop two layers of mesh cut-away stabilizer. Spray the stabilizer with temporary adhesive, and adhere it to the garment, aligning the guide marks. Pin outside of the embroidery field to hold the garment in place, if desired.

**5.** Transfer the daisy design to the machine. Change the needle to a ballpoint needle.

**6.** Place the embroidery hoop on the machine. Make sure that the loose portions of the garment are not under or over the sewing area of the hoop. If needed, roll up the loose edges, and use binder clips or clothespins to secure them.

**7.** Check that the design is centered with the needle in alignment with the design centering mark.

**8.** Use the machine's "fix" or "baste" function, if available, to hold the fabric in place.

**9.** Embroider the design. Refer to the thread chart for correct colors of thread. Clip any jump stitches as you change thread colors. This will prevent the jump stitches from being sewn into the design.

**10.** When embroidery is complete, remove the hoop from the embroidery machine, and remove the garment from the hoop. Remove the excess stabilizer according to the manufacturer's directions. If desired, back the design with fusible knit tricot to protect baby's sensitive skin from irritation.

# Bib Instructions

**1.** Use the same design for this project as you did for the one-piece garment. Center the design on the front of the bib.

**2.** Hoop the paper-release adhesive tear-away stabilizer. Score the inside perimeter of the hoop with a pin, peel away the paper to expose the adhesive, and adhere the bib at the center.

**3.** Place a piece of clear, water-soluble stabilizer over the embroidery field; spray temporary adhesive to hold the stabilizer in place if needed.

**4.** Use the machine's "fix" or "baste" function, if available, to hold the fabric in place.

**5.** Embroider the design. Refer to the Thread and Design Guide for correct colors of thread. Clip any jump stitches as you change thread colors; this will prevent the jump stitches from being sewn into the design.

**6.** When embroidery is complete, remove the hoop from the embroidery machine, and remove the bib from the hoop. Remove the basting stitches, and remove the excess stabilizer following the manufacturer's directions. Any remaining water-soluble stabilizer can be removed during laundering.

# Blanket Instructions

**1.** From the CD-ROM, print out the Thread and Design Guide for the Daisies motif. Place the hoop template over the design template, and trace the outline with the template pencil.

**2.** Lay the blanket out, and use the template to decide where to position the design. For the sample blanket, the design is located on one corner. Once you have the design in position, use the removable marker to mark the hoop placement guides, including the design center point.

**3.** Hoop the paper-release adhesive stabilizer, score the perimeter with a pin, and peel away the paper to expose the adhesive. Align the markings and adhere the blanket.

**4.** Transfer the design to the machine.

**5.** Place the embroidery hoop on the machine. Make sure that the loose portions of the blanket are not under or over the sewing area of the hoop. Roll up the loose edges, and use binder clips or clothespins to secure them.

**6.** Check that the design is centered with the needle in alignment with the design centering mark.

**7.** Use the machine's "fix" or "baste" function, if available, to hold the fabric in place.

**8.** Embroider the design. Refer to the thread chart for correct colors of thread. Clip any jump stitches as you change thread colors; this will prevent the jump stitches from being sewn into the design.

**9.** When embroidery is complete, remove the hoop from the embroidery machine, and remove the blanket from the hoop. Remove the basting stitches and excess stabilizer according to the manufacturer's directions.

# CHAPTER 8
## Irises
### Inviting Irises Dining Accessories

*There is something about an iris that is so durable and hardy.*
*I just love these tall, stately flowers with blossoms*
*that sometimes seem surreal.*
*They are truly a blessing from God.*

*The iris motif adds elegance to any table setting. This tablecloth and napkin set will turn even the most casual luncheon into a garden party.*

## MATERIALS

### Supplies

Round tablecloth, any size

Set of napkins in the desired number

Tear-away stabilizer

Paper-release adhesive tear-away stabilizer

Embroidery thread in periwinkle, blue-violet, navy, white, gold twist, medium avocado, light avocado, dark khaki green and pale green

Bobbin thread

Temporary adhesive

### Tools

General tools listed in Machine Embroidery Basics

### Embroidery Designs

Iris

# Tablecloth Instructions

**1.** From the CD-ROM, print out the Iris design and the Thread and Design Guide. Place the hoop template over the design template, and trace the outline of the Iris with the template pencil.

**2.** Depending upon the size and shape of the tablecloth, locate the approximate placement areas for the design as desired.

**2a. *Round tablecloth:*** For the round tablecloth shown, eight irises were placed around the hem. To find the placement for the irises, fold the cloth in half. Mark the locations for placement by placing a mark on the fold at the hem and another mark about 6" from the hem on both ends of the fold. Re-fold the cloth; bring the marks at the hem together. Mark the new fold line as before. Re-fold the cloth again; this time, match both marks from the previous folds, and mark the fold the same as before. Fold the cloth in half one more time; match the two previous marks. Mark the fold once again. Open the cloth to see the eight markings.

**2b. *Square or rectangular cloth:*** Place one iris in each corner. To properly align the design, fold the corner of the cloth, matching the hems. Place two marks on the fold, one near the hem and the other about 6" above the hem. Repeat this process for all four corners.

**3.** Use a ruler to draw a straight line through both placement marks. Place the template over the line, and align the top and bottom placement guides with the straight line on the fabric. Once you have the design template in position, use the removable marker to mark the hoop placement guides, including the design center point.

**4.** Hoop the tear-away stabilizer and the tablecloth; line up the placement guides. Depending on the fabric weight, you may need more than one layer of stabilizer. Test this first on a similar fabric before beginning embroidery on your tablecloth.

**5.** Transfer the Iris design to the machine.

**6.** Place the embroidery hoop on the machine. Make sure that the loose portions of the cloth are not under or over the sewing area of the hoop; roll up the loose edges, and secure them with clips or clothespins.

**7.** Check that the design is centered with the needle in alignment with the design centering mark.

**8.** Use the machine's "fix" or "baste" function, if available, to hold the fabric in place.

**9.** Embroider the design. Refer to the Thread and Design Guide. Clip any jump stitches as you change thread colors; this will prevent the jump stitches from being sewn into the design.

**2a.**

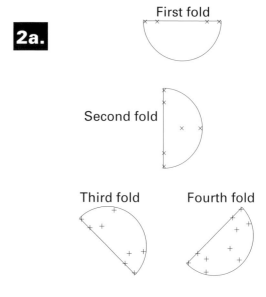

First fold

Second fold

Third fold    Fourth fold

**2b.**

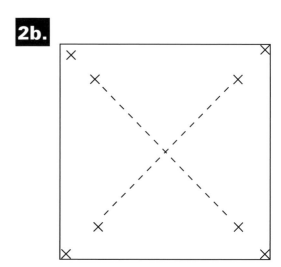

**3.**

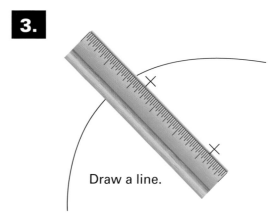

Draw a line.

**10.** When embroidery is complete for the design, remove the hoop from the embroidery machine, and remove the tablecloth from the hoop. Repeat the preparation and embroidery steps to embroider the remaining number of desired designs. When embroidery is complete, remove the basting stitches and excess stabilizer following the manufacturer's directions.

# Napkin Instructions

**1.** Use the printed template to mark the design placement in the desired location.
**2.** Hoop the paper-release adhesive tear-away stabilizer. Score the perimeter of the stabilizer with a pin, and peel away the paper to expose the adhesive. Align the guide marks, and adhere the napkin in place.
**3.** Embroider the design.
**4.** When embroidery is complete, remove the hoop from the embroidery machine, and remove the napkin from the hoop. Remove the basting stitches and excess stabilizer according to the manufacturer's directions. Repeat the preparation and embroidery steps to complete the desired number of napkins.

# CHAPTER 9
# Sweet Peas
## Sweet Pea Bath Towels

*Sweet peas are lacy and girly.*
*Their pink and purple flowers provide*
*a beautiful, feminine accent.*

*Surprise your guests with towels embroidered with pretty sweet peas.*
*The floral motif is perfect for your guest room, as sweet peas symbolize pleasure,*
*bliss and thanksgiving for a lovely time.*

## MATERIALS

### Supplies

Bath towel

Hand towel

Washcloth

Tear-away stabilizer

Paper-release adhesive tear-away stabilizer

Clear, water-soluble stabilizer

Temporary spray adhesive

Embroidery thread in off-white, mauve, petal pink, pastel mauve, bright yellow, mine gold, pale yellow, medium avocado, light avocado, and dark khaki green

Bobbin thread

Temporary adhesive

### Tools

General tools listed in Machine Embroidery Basics

### Embroidery Designs

Sweet Pea

# Bath Towel Instructions

**1.** From the CD-ROM, print out the Thread and Design Guide for the Sweet Pea. Place the hoop template over the design template, and trace the design outline with the template pencil. Lay out the towel, and use the template to decide where to position the design. For the sample towel, the design was centered across the end of the towel. Once the design is in position, use the removable marker to mark the hoop placement guides, including the design center point.

**2.** Hoop the paper-release adhesive stabilizer, score the perimeter with a pin, and peel away the paper to expose the adhesive. Line up the guide marks, and adhere the stabilizer to the towel. Cut a piece of clear, tear-away, water-soluble stabilizer larger than the em-

broidery field. Spray the stabilizer lightly with temporary adhesive, and adhere it to the top of the towel.

**3.** Transfer the Sweet Pea design to the machine.

**4.** Place the embroidery hoop on the machine. Make sure that the loose portions of the towel are not under or over the sewing area of the hoop. Roll up the loose edges, and use binder clips or clothespins to secure them.

**5.** Check that the design is centered with the needle in alignment with the design centering mark.

**6.** Use the machine's "fix" or "baste" function to hold the layers together.

**7.** Embroider the design. Refer to the thread chart for correct colors of thread. Clip any jump stitches as you change thread colors; this will prevent the jump stitches from being sewn into the design.

**8.** When embroidery is complete, remove the hoop from the embroidery machine, and remove the towel from the hoop. Remove the basting stitches and the excess stabilizer from both sides of the towel according to the manufacturer's directions. Any remaining water-soluble stabilizer will be washed away during laundering.

# Hand Towel Instructions

**1.** Follow the same preparation and embroidery instructions as for the bath towel, except use your embroidery machine's software to make the design smaller to fit the hand towel.

**2.** When embroidery is complete, remove the hoop from the embroidery machine, and remove the towel from the hoop. Remove the basting stitches and the excess stabilizer from both sides of the towel according to the manufacturer's directions. Any remaining water-soluble stabilizer will be washed away during laundering.

# Washcloth Instructions

**1.** Re-size the Sweet Pea design to fit the washcloth as desired.

**2.** Cut a piece of paper-release adhesive stabilizer that is slightly larger than the hoop. Score the perimeter of the paper backing with a pin, and peel away the paper to expose the adhesive.

**3.** Use the same method to mark the embroidery design placement. Align the guide marks, and adhere the corner of the washcloth in place on the stabilizer. Cut a piece of clear, water-soluble stabilizer that is slightly larger than the embroidery field. Spray the stabilizer with temporary adhesive, and adhere it on top of the washcloth.

**4.** Place the hoop on the machine. Embroider the design. Refer to the Thread and Design Guide on the CD-ROM for the correct thread colors. Clip any jump stitches as you change thread colors; this will prevent the jump stitches from being sewn into the design.

**5.** When embroidery is complete, remove the hoop from the embroidery machine, and remove the washcloth from the hoop. Remove the basting stitches and the excess stabilizer from both sides of the washcloth according to the manufacturer's directions. Any remaining water-soluble stabilizer will be washed away during laundering.

# CHAPTER 10
## Tulips
### Springtime Sheet Set

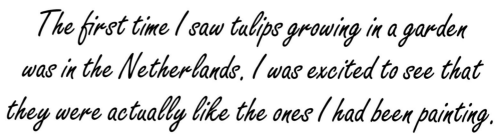

*The first time I saw tulips growing in a garden was in the Netherlands. I was excited to see that they were actually like the ones I had been painting.*

*Imagine sleeping in a field of tulips.*
*You can with these beautiful linens.*

## MATERIALS

### Supplies

Flat sheet

Pillowcase

Medium-weight cut-away stabilizer

Temporary spray adhesive

Embroidery thread in lipstick red, poppy red, orange red, burgundy, medium avocado, light avocado and dark khaki green

Bobbin thread

Temporary adhesive

### Tools

General tools listed in Machine Embroidery Basics

### Embroidery Designs

Tulips

## Sheet Instructions

**1.** Use the re-sizing feature in embroidery software or at the machine screen to reduce the size of the Tulips design. Use the machine functions or software to reduce the design to fit onto the hemmed area of the sheet. Print out the Thread and Design Guide on the CD-ROM.

**2.** Place the hoop template over the design template, and trace the outline with the template pencil. Lay the sheet out. Use the template to position the tulips on the sheet and determine how many repeats will be needed. Choose the direction to position the tulips. Once the design is in position, use the removable marker to mark the vertical and horizontal placement guides and the design center point.

**3.** Hoop the cut-away stabilizer, spray it with temporary adhesive and adhere the sheet, aligning the guide marks. Before embroidering on your sheet, run a test on similar fabric to see if you need more than one layer of stabilizer. With dense designs and lighter-weight fabrics, two layers often are required.

**4.** Transfer the desired Tulips design to the machine.

**5.** Place the embroidery hoop on the machine. Make sure that the loose portions of the sheet are not under or over the sewing area of the hoop. Roll up the loose edges, and use binder clips or clothespins to secure them.

**6.** Check that the design is centered with the needle in alignment with the design centering mark.

**7.** Use the machine's "fix" or "baste" function, if available, to hold the fabric in place. Otherwise pin carefully or hand-baste outside of the embroidery field.

**8.** Embroider the design. Refer to the Thread and Design Guide for the correct colors of thread. Clip any jump stitches as you change thread colors. This will prevent the jump stitches from being sewn into the design.

**9.** Repeat the steps as desired to create a border along the top of the sheet. If available, use software and a larger hoop to save time.

**10.** When embroidery is complete, remove the hoop from the embroidery machine, and remove the sheet from the hoop. Remove the basting stitches and the excess stabilizer according to the manufacturer's directions.

# Pillowcase Instructions

**1.** Follow the general preparation and embroidery instructions given for the sheet. Depending upon the width of the pillowcase hem, you may need to adjust the size of the design to fit it better. Place the designs as desired. For the sample pillowcase, a single tulip was placed so that it will be viewed vertically when the pillow is placed on the bed.

**2.** When embroidery is complete, remove the hoop from the embroidery machine, and remove the pillowcase from the hoop. Remove the basting stitches and the excess stabilizer according to the manufacturer's directions.

# BONUS PROJECTS ON THE CD-ROM

*Step-by-step instructions for the following additional projects are included in PDF files on the CD-ROM, which is attached to this book's back cover.*

**Rose and Damselfly
Capri Set**

**Hydrangea and Butterfly
Dress Set**

**Rose and Sweet Pea
T-shirt Dress**

**Classic Cardigan with
Hydrangea Brooch**

**Rose Kitchen Set**

**Beautiful Butterflies
Ensemble**

**Bag of Blue**

**Coming Up Daisies
Garden Set**

# CONTRIBUTORS

*All of the embroidery designs featured in this book are included on the CD-ROM located inside the book's back cover. Cactus Punch digitized the designs from Donna Dewberry's original artwork. Additional Donna Dewberry Embroidery Designs by Cactus Punch are available at your local retailer or online at www.onestitchquilting.com.*

## Badger Basket Co.

Manufacturer of toy and juvenile furniture, including the Moses basket featured in the photography

P.O. Box 227
Edgar, WI 54426
Phone: (800) 236-1310
Web: www.badgerbasket.com

## Cactus Punch

Digitizer of machine embroidery designs, including others from Donna Dewberry Designs

4955 N. Shamrock Place
Tucson, AZ 85705
Phone: (800) 487-6972
Web: www.cactus-punch.com

## Dewberry Designs Inc.

Source for Donna Dewberry products, including books, fabrics, embroidery designs and more

355 Citrus Tower Blvd. Suite 104
Clermont, FL 34711
Phone: (800) 536-2627
E-mail: e-mail@onestroke.com
Web: www.onestitchquilting.com

## Furniture and Appliance Mart Superstore

Retailer of name-brand furniture, appliances, electronics and bedding, and provider of photo shoot location

3349 Church St.
Stevens Point, WI 54481
Phone: (715) 344-7700
Web: www.furnitureappliancemart.com

## Golden Eagle Log Homes

Manufacturer of quality log homes and provider of photo shoot location

4421 Plover Road
Wisconsin Rapids, WI 54494
Phone: (800) 270-5025
E-mail: goldnegl@wctc.net
Web: www.goldeneagleloghomes.com

## Krause Publications

Publisher of quality how-to books on machine embroidery, quilting, sewing and other crafts

700 E. State St.
Iola, WI 54990
Phone: (888) 457-2873
Web: www.krause.com

## Prym Consumer USA

Manufacturer of sewing, quilting, cutting and craft-related tools and notions

P.O. Box 5028
Spartanburg, SC 29304
Web: www.dritz.com

## Springs Creative Products Group

Manufacturer of coordinated home furnishings, bed and bath products, and home sewing and quilting fabrics, including Donna Dewberry's Quilting Basics line of fabrics used to create the Bag of Blue

P.O. Box 10232
Rock Hill, SC 29731
Phone: (800) 234-6688
Web: www.springscreativeproductsgroup.com

## Sulky of America, Inc.

Manufacturer of threads, stabilizers and spray adhesives, including the thread, stabilizers and KK2000 temporary spray adhesive used to make the projects shown in this book

P.O. Box 494129
Port Charlotte, FL 33949-4129
Phone: (800) 874-4115
E-mail: info@sulky.com
Web: www.sulky.com

## VSM Sewing Inc.

Manufacturer of sewing and embroidery machines, including the machines used to create the projects in this book

31000 Viking Parkway
Westlake, OH 44145
Phone: (800) 358-0001
E-mail: info@husqvarnaviking.com
Web: www.husqvarnaviking.com

# RESOURCES

### Embroidery Machines

Baby Lock
Web: www.babylock.com

Bernina
Web: www.berninausa.com

Brother
Web: www.brother.com

Elna
Web: www.elnausa.com

Janome
Web: www.janome.com

Kenmore
Web: www.sears.com

Pfaff
Web: www.pfaff.com

Simplicity
Web: www.simplicitysewing.com

Singer
Web: www.singershop.com

Viking Sewing Machines
Web: www.husqvarnaviking.com

White
Web: www.whitesewing.com

### Embroidery Publications

Creative Machine Embroidery
Web: www.cmemag.com

Designs in Machine Embroidery
Web: www.dzgns.com

Embroidery Journal
Web: www.embroideryjournal.com

### General Notions and Supplies

Clotilde LLC
Web: www.clotilde.com

Ghee's
Web: www.ghees.com

Nancy's Notions
Web: www.nancysnotions.com

# MORE CREATIVE USES
## for Your Embroidery Machine

### Embroidery Machine Essentials:
### Appliqué Adventures
**Companion Project Series: Book 6**

by Mary Mulari

Create 13 beautiful appliqué projects to add a personal touch to any quilt, garment or paper gift, using the detailed instructions and 40 embroidery designs in this book and accompanying CD-ROM.

Softcover • 8¼ x 10⅞ • 48 pages
100+ color photos and illus.
**Item# Z0314 • $22.99**

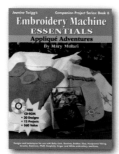

### Contemporary Machine Embroidered Fashions
**Transform Everyday Garments**
**into Designer Originals**

by Eileen Roche

Transform your wardrobe using machine embroidery to add stylish touches to 20 projects, including jeans, Capri pants and jackets, covered in 30 designs on an included CD-ROM.

Softcover • 8¼ x 10⅞ • 144 pages
125+ color photos and illus.
**Item# MEFF • $29.99**

### Machine Embroidery Wild & Wacky
**Stitch on Any and Every Surface**

by Linda Griepentrog and Rebecca Kemp Brent

Go beyond machine embroidery basics using unique bases such as wood and canvas, and techniques including embossing and painting, and apply to 28 projects on a bonus CD-ROM.

Softcover • 8¼ x 10⅞ • 128 pages
225 color photos and illus.
**Item# MEWA • $29.99**

### Embroidery Machine Essentials:
### Piecing Techniques
**Companion Project Series: Book 5**

by Jeanine Twigg

Jeanine Twigg continues her popular series with this innovative machine embroidery piecing techniques book. With 12 home décor projects and accessories, plus a CD-ROM with 60 designs, this book more than pays for itself.

Softcover • 8¼ x 10⅞ • 48 pages
75 color photos, 75 illus.
**Item# EMEP • $19.99**

### Machine Embroidery on Paper

by Annette Gentry Bailey

This exciting reference takes machine embroidery into paper crafts with 30+ cool embroidered projects including cards, frames, boxes and sachets. Features 20 original embroidery designs on an enclosed CD-ROM.

Softcover • 8¼ x 10⅞ • 48 pages
115+ color photos and illus.
**Item# MEPP • $22.99**

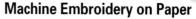

### Machine Embroidery Room by Room
**30+ Home Décor Projects**

by Carol Zentgraf

Tackle a small-scale home makeover with themes and three design groupings for eight unique rooms, featured in 30+ projects. The CD-ROM includes 50 exclusive embroidery designs and a bonus monogram in 2 sizes.

Softcover • 8¼ x 10⅞ • 128 pages
200+ color photos and illus.
**Item# MEHD • $29.99**

### Machine Embroidery With Confidence
**A Beginner's Guide**

by Nancy Zieman

Nancy Zieman explains the basics of machine embroidery including what tools to use, how to organize the embroidery area, types of machines, designs, templating/positioning, software, stabilizers, troubleshooting and finishing touches.

Softcover • 8¼ x 10⅞ • 128 pages
100 color photos
**Item# CFEM • $21.99**

### Contemporary Machine Embroidered Quilts
**Innovative Techniques and Designs**

by Eileen Roche

Moves from the basics of material selection and design, to 12 fabulous projects that combine quilting and embroidery. Patterns for quilts and embroidery designs are included on a free CD-ROM.

Softcover • 8¼ x 10⅞ • 144 pages
75 color photos, 75 illus., plus CD inserted
**Item# MEQ • $27.99**

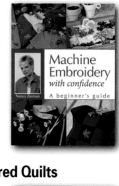

**To order call 800-258-0929 Offer CRB6**
Krause Publications, Offer CRB6
P.O. Box 5009, Iola WI 54945-5009
www.krausebooks.com

Please add $4.00 for the first book and $2.25 each additional for shipping & handling to U.S. addresses. Non-U.S. addresses please add $20.95 for the first book and $5.95 each additional.
Residents of CA, IA, IL, KS, NJ, PA, SD, TN, VA, WI please add appropriate sales tax.